acquisition of wealth and property matter? Where nothing else is important?

If someone were to kill this author I would not shed a tear. Beat him with a stick and take the money out of HIS pocket and then see if he likes it.

Jesus said we should be kind to our fellow man. This writer says we should lie to our fellow man, betray him and take his money. What kind of advice is this?

Not even a desperate man would consider the advice offered in this book.

Finally, someone wrote down what some knew and what everybody should know.

Praise for
THE GRAMMAR OF MONEY

WHAT KIND OF MONSTER could write this kind of garbage, urging people to steal, cheat and betray each other?

Who wrote this book? It would be best for everyone if all copies were seized and burnt, and all computer files hunted down and deleted. A work like this should not be permitted to survive.

Dear Andalus, I don't know what you expect me to say about this horrible, aggressive work. The author is in favor of crimes of all kinds and shows no humanity whatsoever. I would return the book to you but then you might send it to someone else. I am afraid to throw it in the trash because someone might pick it out. Therefore I am ripping the binding off and putting it in as shredder. If I could kill it with fire, I would.

The pseudonymous author of this evil text is a wretched human being. He throws off all the cardinal virtues in an attempt to replace them with his own evil thoughts. This author would not only steal from a blind man but would praise others who would try to do the same.

Unbridled capitalism and greed at its worst.

The undisciplined pursuit of wealth is praised in a book that I would be ashamed to be seen with in public.

In former times, authors such as those who wrote *The Grammar of Money* were burned at the stake, and rightly so.

They say that sunlight is the best disinfectant, but in this case the philosophy of money must be suppressed and its author imprisoned.

"Do unto others," the Good Book commands. "Fuck them," counsels *The Grammar of Money*. A truly wretched book.

I have nothing to say on a positive note about this book. Please take me off your reading list.

Calling Christ and St. Francis of Assisi naive will win this author no fans. His God is money.

If I could find the author of this so-called "work," I would punch him in the face.

We were placed on this planet not to do good, but to acquire wealth. It's all about the money. So says the evil author of this book. He should be denounced from every pulpit in the country.

Have we come to this? Where nothing but the

THE GRAMMAR OF MONEY

Rules and Commentary

FELOUZ

ANDALUS
PUBLISHING

Copyright © 2020 by Andalus Publishing.

All rights reserved.

No part of this book may be reproduced in any form or by any electronic or mechanical means, including information storage and retrieval systems, without written permission from the publisher, except for the use of brief quotations in a book review.

ISBN: 978-1-945979-16-3 (paperback)
ISBN 978-1-945979-17-0 (ePub)

 Created with Vellum

1

Introduction

Money is a foreign language. Like any language, money has a grammar with rules to be learned. No one will understand if you try to speak without grammar. To understand money, you must understand its rules. To be successful with money you must learn its grammar.

This book attempts to teach the long-hidden rules of money. Taken from both historical and popular sources across a range of cultures, this book lays out the rules you need to know about money and power.

If you don't want to be poor, you must learn the grammar of money. This book teaches you the vocabulary and rules you need to know to be successful. If you do not understand the grammar of money someone will take your money from you. Take his away first, if you can.

What is money? The phrase, "a medium of exchange" begs a more comprehensive answer.

In fact, there is no single, comprehensive definition.

What about dollars? Dollars are the world's reserve currency, but the value of a dollar must be measured in terms of some other store of value, and there is no permanent store of value. Today, a dollar may be 1/100th of a barrel of Brent crude oil, but tomorrow that number may change.

What about gold? Historically, gold has been a reliable medium of exchange and store of value, but gold is no longer money. In the 1930's, the US even made it illegal to own gold. In terms of dollars, its value is always fluctuating.

So what is money? Money is belief. Money, John Buchan claimed, is frozen desire. For money to exist, we must all agree that it exists. Everyone agrees that play money is not real money. If you find yourself in a situation where money is banned, money can be anything. Prisoners are forbidden cash in prison, so in jail, cigarets can be money. Anything can be money, as long as there is general agreement.

Money is created. There are times when the money supply shrinks or expands, but usually, money is a zero sum game. "Money has no grey areas," Kevin O'Leary of *Shark Tank* said. "You either make it or lose it." If I have it, you do not. If you have it, I do not. We both cannot hold the same money.

No one supplies you with money. You must

take the money owed to you. You can decide to exchange your services or other things of value, but money will not rain upon you from the sky.

Business is based on the exchange of money. All business is deception and theft. You never tell your customer your true cost. Retailers pay little for an item compared to what their retail customers pay, but the wholesalers or manufacturers who sell to retailers pay even less. So what is the true price of an item? What a buyer is willing to pay. What is a fair price? What a buyer is willing to pay. What is an unfair price? What a buyer has paid before learning that someone else paid less.

Since the 1980's, money has been weaponized. Economic sanctions prevent the transfer of money in certain kinds of transactions. You can no longer legally spend cash over certain amounts without complying with reporting regulations governing the transfer of cash. Eventually, such compliance will be required over all transactions that meet the threshold, whether they are conducted in cash or not. The "cashless society" is wonderful news for regulators. Cash is anonymous.

Money must be controlled. The traditional justifications are always trotted out: "to protect society," "to reduce crime" and so forth. Money outside the banking system is slowly disappearing while money inside the system is subject to strict controls and confiscation. Paper gains and paper losses are not truly money because they have not been reduced to cash. Home equity can disappear in an instant. Cash inside the banking system can be taken at any time.

Whenever you acquire a good deal of money, prepare for the consequences. Someone always turns up claiming to be a creditor. A relative suddenly needs cash. The government has its tax hand out. If realizing a great deal of money was only a question of paying taxes owed, you would simply pay and be done with it. But there is always something else. Always.

There is always someone willing and happy to take your money, whether disguised as a hedge funds manager, an advisor, a consultant, a lawyer, a girlfriend, a wife or a husband. If you do not understand this you will not be able to keep your money for long.

Traditional morality is of no use here. Christian schoolchildren are taught to admire the poor and their savior was an itinerant prophet who tried—unsuccessfully—to throw money out of the churches. No one knows where the custom of donating money to religions started, but at least by the time of Ancient Egypt it was well-established. Money given for the repair of an earthly temple would insure better treatment in the afterlife.

Success in business is not shameful in Islam. Before he started his mission, the Prophet Mohammed was a businessman. Buddhist monks swear an oath of poverty but walk the streets each morning to collect what amounts to a food tax from believers who hope for better treatment in the afterlife. Joseph Smith, the prophet of the Mormons, knew that banks create money and so started one.

Unfortunately, he did not have a solution to the problem of what to so when there is a run on the bank and his bank failed. It would be more than a century and a half before a solution proposed by the economist Milton Friedman would be tested. But Friedman's solution would not work unless and until money became divorced from any asset or store of value and became pure frozen desire. That kind of money, like faith, is infinite.

If you worship the poor you will become poor yourself. If you despise money you will never have enough of it. If seek to acquire as much as you can, you may fail and not meet your goals, but at least you will have more money than the person who doesn't bother.

If you become wealthy and decide to contribute to the poor, keep in mind that there are good reasons to do so, reasons beyond having your name prominently displayed on a new—or existing—hospital wing or research institute. The rich are treated well in this life and those who have enough to spread their wealth are treated the best of all for the simple reason that good treatment always comes with the hope that some of that wealth will shared.

There is no point at all in being cruel to the

wealthy, unless you are already wealthy yourself. Even then, it makes little sense, because you never know when you will be in some kind of a financial jam of one kind or another and need a lifeline. Poor friends won't be able to help out.

2

General Rules

MONEY IS EVERYTHING. • NOTHING IS MORE IMPORTANT THAN MONEY. • MONEY HAS NO MORALITY. • MONEY IS POWER. • MONEY IS FROZEN DESIRE. • MONEY IS FAITH. • GREED IS AN ILLUSION. • GREED IS ETERNAL. • PROFIT IS ITS OWN REWARD. • ANYTHING WORTH DOING IS WORTH DOING FOR MONEY. • IT'S ALWAYS ABOUT THE MONEY.

I DON'T KNOW if God exists, but money does.

Philosophers argue over the existence of God but no one argues over the existence of money.

People may worship different gods but everyone worships money. When it comes to money, there is only one religion.

NOTHING IS as important as money. What comes before or what comes after death is a subject of debate. In this life, nothing is more important. No one debates the existence of money. Money simply is. If you try to define it, the definition will slip through your fingers. Everyone knows what is and what is not money. Money is not an item of value, money is value itself.

Man's god is money, the god of the here and now; of desire, of gratification, of fulfillment. But though many study money, the truth of money and its secret rules are just beyond their grasp. Money doesn't care what you think. Money is you over the other guy or the other guy over you. Money is helping yourself, money is helping others with the goal of helping yourself.

Money has no shame. Do not let others take away your money. Take theirs away first.

As we condemn those who pursue money, we ourselves are drawn to its pursuit. We cannot help ourselves. There is nothing as important as money in the world.

Preachers condemn those who would make money into a god, but where there is no God there still is money. No pursuit, no avocation is as important as the pursuit of money.

THERE IS a strong taboo surrounding money. It is socially forbidden to discuss how much one earns, except in specialized contexts designed for the exchange of such information. At any other kind of social gathering, asking someone how much someone earns is considered rude behavior. Americans are much more comfortable discussing their sexual peculiarities than their take-home pay. Whenever these discussions do start, there is no reason why the information exchanged should be believed.

People boast about how much money they make. They exaggerate. They claim to own leased assets. They assert that they have more money than they do. The only time people exaggerate how little they have is when they are asked for a loan. When asked for money, not even the well off are well-off. "My money's tied up in CD's." "I'd like to but I'm not liquid enough." These are examples of the kind of excuses proffered by the rich as a polite way to deflect beggars.

The person who boasts of how much money he has does not usually have anything of significance. A person may boast of his deal-making prowess–Trump comes to mind–but soon after you learn he is no stranger to the bankruptcy court.

People who play for high stakes can win big, but they can also lose big. Keep this in mind whenever you are tempted to roll the dice. Never let the failure of a business transaction leave you in penury. Use bankruptcy as a tactical maneuver to free yourself of bad debts so that you can take on risks again. Never give personal guarantees. Never lend money without the loan becoming an investment. All of these ideas are elementary, basic concepts of the grammar of money.

Though these subjects are taboo, they are nevertheless discussed in subtle ways. Designer marks are popular because it is a discreet way to advertise your own exclusivity. Club memberships are similar. Attending events sold out long ago, flying private jets using the off-terminal general aviation area of the airport—all of these telegraph wealth. Remember that nothing can break you more quickly than trying to keep up with the truly wealthy. Unless you are in the billionaire class, you have no idea how much these frills cost. Even those in the billionaire class are not aware—they pay people to stay on top of what for them are mundane expenses.

F. SCOTT FITZGERALD famously pointed out that the rich are different. Indeed they are. The rich can buy whatever they want. The truly rich can even buy extended life. The truly rich have a different decision-making process. A trifle for a billionaire is a life-changing matter even for a wealthy millionaire. You may think that with 10 million dollars you are wealthy, but it was Tom

Wolfe who pointed out that at ten million, after adding up the cost of a condo in Manhattan, the weekend home in the Hamptons, the ski lodge in Aspen, and the jet to get there, when all is said and done there is little left in the pocket.

The rich are lonely because they loathe interaction with people who will inevitably ask them for money. Unlike those who recently acquired money, they dress shabbily to avoid these interactions. Except for their shoes, of course.

The consequence of this shunning is that they become lonely. If there is any characteristic common amongst the wealthy it is loneliness. Billionaires and the nobility congregate to commiserate over their shared problems. No one else understands. The poor are not hounded by the press.

The only time the rich can relax is when no one knows who they are or when they are amongst their own.

Go to where the money is. If you want to find real money it helps to be in places where money is found. Suter's Mill in 1848. Silicon Valley today. Wall Street. The City of London. Geneva. The Turkish Republic of Northern Cyprus. Beirut. If you can't get to any of these places, look to those places in your own country where finance is king. Bay Street, Toronto. LaSalle Street, Chicago. Olaya Street in Riyadh.

At first you may only get the drips and dregs, the crumbs that only occasionally fall from the tables of the rich. But it is better than your miserable, poor, empty pocket, hand to mouth existence elsewhere. You won't get lucky unless and until you put yourself in a position to take advantage of any luck that may come to you. Worshipping in the cathedrals of cash can bring benefits, benefits that you won't see elsewhere.

Buy, beg, borrow or steal—does it really matter?—a way out. If you are trapped, it may be the only way. Eventually debts will be forgotten or forgiven. Money that is stolen, even large amounts—perhaps especially large amounts, is quickly written off. Money that is given to you as a gift is yours and does not need to be returned. If you are in circumstances with no clear path to profit, get out and get out fast.

Excuses for inaction are many and so often stated with eloquence. "I can't follow any of these concepts because I don't have enough money." "I can't move." "I have to take the kids to school." "I can't find a new apartment that takes pets."

Don't let details keep you from moving forward. Jettison the limiting conditions or resign yourself that you will never be rich. If you truly cannot change your circumstances, at least try to take advantage within your own small sphere. Exploit and take advantage of all those you come into contact with.

Whether you realize it or not, they are trying to take advantage of you. It is a cutthroat world. If you are not the predator, you are the prey.

You put yourself into this situation. Or you were born into it. It makes no difference. Getting out may be painful, but you can get out.

It is difficult to teach people the importance of money because no many other currents in society teach the opposite: forbearance, how true value is unrelated to money, how money isn't everything, how money isn't really that important.

These same teachers are never around when there are bills to pay though they are first in line when anyone offers a handout. The fact is, without money all those nice things are or soon will be unavailable. Two can live as cheaply as one, the saying goes, but without money neither will be able to live at all.

Subsistence farming is no longer a reality. This means that money is a question of life and death. Money is a question of survival. Without money you die. It's that simple. Eventually you'll die anyway, but without money you'll die a lot sooner.

People who are fluent in money are not prized at a young age. There are no awards for making or saving money. High school letterman sweaters aren't given to those who read the *Wall Street Journal*. It is only later that society adulates the successful.

The pursuit of wealth is glorious, said Deng Xiao Ping, whose influence on the People's Republic of China was great because he turned the country away from economic Communism and let China earn.

Mao's suppression of what is today called "Chinese characteristics," i.e., capitalism, was a mistake. Until unrestrained capitalism and the greedy pursuit of wealth were unleashed, China struggled to pull itself up by its bootstraps, a fate shared by so many developing nations that failed to put the pursuit of money over all else.

Reduce taxes, declare a free zone and let your people pursue wealth at any cost, free of all restrictions. This is the only path to wealth and prosperity. If that means stepping on the toes of other nations, so be it. If it means someone loses, so be it. Let those who believe in the Golden Rule do unto others while you fill your pockets.

The British writer Somerset Maugham wrote that "Money is like a sixth sense without which you cannot make a complete use of the other five." Money is essential. Money is all.

3

Customers

Don't tell customers more than they need to know. • Learn the customer's weaknesses, so that you can better take advantage. • Beware the customer's thirst for knowledge. • All sellers are motivated. • Cherish good customers. • An angry customer is an enemy, and a satisfied customer is an ally. • It's always good business to know about new customers before they walk in your door. • Never cheat a customer unless you can get away with it. • A paying enemy is a customer. • Always help fools part with their money. • Only fools pay retail. • If you can't recognize the sucker at the table, you are the sucker.

THESE ARE general rules of behavior in all sales situations. An educated customer is only a good customer to the extent that he does not know what your cost is. The minute he learns your cost, he will ask for a larger discount, so beware of a customer's eagerness to learn more about whatever it is that you are selling, whether it is a product or a service. Learning about your customer's needs is important if you are going to make a sale. Knowing how much money you customer has will make it easier to take it from him.

Your own eagerness for knowledge should always be greater than that of a greedy customer. An angry customer who still does business with you would probably go elsewhere if he could. Keep this in mind when you raise prices to take advantage of his predicament.

There are laws about warranties and hidden defects. People do not generally know the terms of these laws, other than the fact that they exist. There is a natural tendency to trust printed forms. Take advantage of this trust and spell out lesser protections than what the law provides for. People will usually believe your misleading form if printed. If you want to provide greater protections than the law's bare minimums, charge for them.

There is no such thing as a "fair price." There is only the price that the customer is willing to pay, and at which you are willing to part with your merchandise. Price is malleable, ever changing: a change in circumstances can make worthless items more precious than rubies.

A freak snowstorm is all it takes to increase the value of snow shovels gathering dust in the corner of a store.

A wholesaler sells at wholesale prices and makes a comfortable profit. Why then, should you pay retail, especially if the retailer adds no value? Drop-shippers are particularly at risk; what value can they possibly provide?

The final rule here is from the film *Rounders*, and is a well-known poker mainstay. If you can't recognize the fool, you are the fool. Remember this rule in a business transaction when you are unsure and fear that you might be taken advantage of. It costs nothing to get up and walk away.

Often, this is the best course. There is no such thing as "today only" or "limited time." Once negotiations truly begin, everything is on the table.

4

Family and Friends

PROFIT BEFORE FAMILY. • EXPLOITATION BEGINS AT HOME. • NEVER PLACE FRIENDSHIP ABOVE PROFIT. • TREAT PEOPLE IN YOUR DEBT LIKE FAMILY: EXPLOIT THEM. • EVERYTHING IS FOR SALE, EVEN FRIENDSHIP. • BEWARE OF FALSE PARTNERS. • EVERY MAN HAS HIS PRICE. • KNOW YOUR ENEMIES AND DO BUSINESS WITH THEM. • TRUST NO ONE. • ALWAYS PUT MONEY OVER FRIENDSHIP; FRIENDSHIP RARELY BRINGS MONEY. • IF YOU WANT A FRIEND, GET A DOG.

"BETRAYAL," sang Phish, "begins with trust." Friendship is risk. As Rick said in the film *Casablanca*, "I stick my neck out for nobody." Donald Trump taught his children, "Don't trust anyone." Only those who are close can betray you. The closer they are, the worse the betrayal. When it comes to money there is no trust.

Do not think that family is incapable of betrayal either. Family members believe themselves immune. If you cannot trust family, whom can you trust? You are more likely to be betrayed by a family member than an acquaintance for the simple fact that with family, you let your guard down. Family finds it easy to betray you because they know your secrets. Anyone who knows you for a long time will learn your secrets, no matter how hard you try to conceal them. Mere acquaintances are not so informed.

Everyone is wary of strangers, and with good reason. Casual chit-chat always has an agenda if it lasts for more than a few minutes. You will rarely have enough time during the initial encounter to discern what that agenda is, but nevertheless it is there. Assume that it is about money, even if the donation-seeker on the street offers freebies and an assurance that the exchange isn't about money at all; it's about the whales or the elephants or our city's need for two symphony orchestras, but in the end it comes down to money.

It is always about the money. Always. When they say it is not about the money, that should be a lit-up electric billboard soaring a thousand feet hight saying "It's about the money."

Ted Kaczynski, the Unabomber, successfully evaded the FBI's nationwide manhunt for years. It was his brother who turned him in.

A retired woman chatting to friends at a beauty parlor mentioned to them an incident in

Chicago, thirty years ago, that ended in murder. One of those friends mentioned the incident to the police, and sure enough, there was an open murder case that roughly fit the details the acquaintance heard while getting her hair done. The arrest came shortly thereafter.

This betrayal grew out of a casual conversation. Kaczynski's betrayal was so much worse, coming from a family member. A family member knows your foibles, that your lame alibi is just that or that a relationship you boasted of never existed. Your relatives knew you before you long before you became wealthy and they are all uncomfortable with your new status. That status may be familiar to everyone who knows you and who knows of you, but it is unfamiliar to your family.

It is not easy to keep secrets from a spouse. Keeping secrets from a spouse is mentally taxing. There is what was supposed to happen, what actually happened, and what you told your spouse happened. All of this means that a single incident will have three versions. Multiply this by the days of the week, the months of the year and it will be simply too much to get straight, too much to remember.

You will be reduced to saying, "but that happened so long ago," a pathetic excuse when for your spouse, the incident might as well have happened yesterday. And God forbid if you have to change your story to accommodate new facts. Every single subparagraph and point of your previous lie will be thrown at you. You won't be able to weave a story that contains both the truth and all your lies.

This is why people are driven to murder. They sail from calm waters, slowly making waves to a complete and utter shipwreck in just a few days They haven't had the time to understand the ramifications of everything that has happened and can't quite figure a way out. The easiest answer is to eliminate the irritant, the troublemaker, but in their confused state of mind they fail to realize that murder is not easy and will just bring another more complicated set of problems

A partner knows where the bodies are buried. Betray a partner and run the risk that all of them will be unearthed. Do not estimate the appetite for self-destruction when it becomes to betrayal either: "if she were to tell the company about my skimming I would lose my job and maybe go to jail and then there would be no money for her. So she would not do that." Oh yes, she would.

While you are explaining your naive belief to a lawyer, bartender, or anyone else who would listen, she is already on the phone to the authorities or her own lawyer because she doesn't care about you, she just wants revenge, she just wants to get even. Anger can get in the way of money. It won't be for a good long while until she realizes that her betrayal has killed the golden goose and now there is no money left for anyone.

Anger is like that; it blinds people to the consequences, and consequences are always financial.

There are some things you must hide from a partner in case of trouble, financial or domestic. The days of secret bank accounts are over. All bank accounts, because of "Know Your Customer" rules, are linked to a personal ID number and can be retrieved with a subpoena.

Seek to have no long term friends. You don't need them. Friends are an expense. And long term friends will think nothing of asking you for money where a mere acquaintance might be afraid to do so.

If you are lonely, rent friends. Never buy them. When you stop paying, they will go away, which is exactly what you want. They won't come around anymore once they realize that the money is gone and isn't coming back. You cannot purchase new relatives but this is probably a good thing. If anyone asks, a sob story about how you were an only child and your parents are dead halts meddlesome inquiries.

As a general rule, you cannot afford to have friends. Friends should be kept at a distance. They should never be privy to your business affairs. Having friends is a luxury. If you must have friends, cycle through them every three years or so. Friends are a risk and to be successful, risks need to be eliminated.

5

Honor

A MAN WITH NO MONEY IS NO MAN AT ALL. • THERE IS NO HONOR IN POVERTY. • HOPE DOESN'T PAY THE BILLS. • A MAN WITH AN EMPTY POCKET AND HIS DIGNITY HAS AN EMPTY POCKET. • A POOR MAN WHO STILL HAS HIS PRIDE IS A POOR MAN. • LET OTHERS KEEP THEIR REPUTATION. YOU KEEP THEIR MONEY. • MORALITY IS WHAT IS COST-EFFECTIVE. • HE WHO LOSES HIS MONEY LOSES ALL. • A MAN IS ONLY WORTH THE SUM OF HIS POSSESSIONS.

THERE IS no honor in poverty. A poor person must beg in order to survive. Thoughts and prayers do not get bills paid. Action and work does. Thinking about problems does not solve them. The only way you will free yourself from money worries is by obtaining more money.

Money is the lifeblood of society. Without

money, people die. The government's promises to help the poor and the homeless are just that: promises. Promises do not pay bills. Promises are not checks that can be cashed.

The loss of a job is catastrophic for most people. The fact of termination and the humiliation of being separated from company service, is nothing compared to the loss of a regular paycheck.

Not so long ago, a person who was fired would simply go out and get a new job. Those days are long gone. Jobs are not easy to come by. Your most valuable asset is your job—or your business. The loss of income is a crisis, whether the loss hits you at age 25 or 65. You will never be prepared for it. If you lose your money you lose everything.

The only true solution is to get more money, by any means necessary. Living on the street is a real threat. Don't let it happen to you. Don't let your pride stand in the way of your money. Money comes first, pride second or third if at all. A humiliating job that pays is still a job. It doesn't matter how you fill your pocket with money as long as your pocket is full.

A man without money is a woeful creature, trapped, a parasite with no way to get anywhere, reduced to 19th century distances because he cannot even afford bus fare. His clothes slowly deteriorate because he can buy no replacements and sleeping on concrete or cardboard is tough on fabric. He gets ill because he cannot afford to see a doctor. Unless he can bathe in the ocean in warm weather, he will start to smell gamey because there are few free bathing facilities available to the homeless. He is thrown out of public libraries and threatened with arrest for trying to freshen up there. Wherever he goes there is no opportunity, no help, no hope in this wonderful beacon of liberty that is the United States of America.

6

Law

WITH MONEY, LAWS CAN BE CHANGED. • JUSTICE DELAYED IS JUSTICE ACHIEVED. • STRIVE TO BE JUDGMENT PROOF. • POSSESSION IS OWNERSHIP. • PARDONS CAN BE PURCHASED. • ALL SINS ARE FORGIVEN ONCE YOU START MAKING A LOT OF MONEY. • MONEY IS ALWAYS THE REASON FOR WAR. • VENGEANCE IS A LUXURY.

THOSE WHO PRAISE the Rule of Law and how all men are equal before the law are utterly naive. If the wealthy do not like a law they pay to get it changed. If there is not enough time to change the law, there is still time to contribute to the election coffers of judges to insure that only friendly jurists sit on the bench.

Judges who are elected must obtain their campaign funds from somewhere—they are not paid enough to finance political campaigns from their salary alone. It is much easier to buy politicians. Politicians are always running for office. They solicit campaign contributions in a much more open fashion.

Money buys access, and access can be turned into sponsorship of needed legislation. The Rule of Law is for others, not for you. If you don't like the laws, change them. That is what the wealthy do.

And what of the criminal law? Ordinary defendants are heaped together onto judicial calendars that may or may not be heard at the scheduled time and are much more likely to have their cases continued. The wealthy and their lawyers who contributed to the judge's campaign are heard first. Lawyers who did not contribute come afterwards and the poor defendants always come last.

LITIGATION IS DISRUPTIVE CIVIL WARFARE. Knowing Sun Tzu's *Art of War* is just as important, if not more important, than familiarity with the Rules of Civil Procedure.

There are many ways to make cases go away. Delay is chief amongst them, and there is no single event or milestone designed to mark progress in a trial that cannot be delayed.

All cases can be delayed. For example, consider the following. Civil cases begin with the filing of a document called a "Complaint." According to the rules, this document should be followed by another document called an "Answer."

This rarely happens. Instead, attorneys respond to the Complaint with a "Motion to Enlarge Time," that is, a motion for a continuance. This should be repeated at least once, and perhaps twice. The next document to be filed is a "Motion to Dismiss," followed by another, if the rules permit, each followed by another Motion to Enlarge Time.

In this way a process that should take no longer than thirty days can be stretched out for six months or more. This is why civil cases can often consume half a decade and by that time the original reasons for the lawsuit no longer apply or are forgotten, or the person prosecuting the case has moved on or died. Justice delayed, if you are a civil defendant, is justice achieved.

PEOPLE BELIEVE in the delusion that all they have to do to obtain money from another in the judicial system is to win their case. This is magical thinking.

In fact, there are but a few instances where judgment debtors are immediately forced to pay. Failure to pay child support is one of them; failure to pay federal taxes another. In almost every other situation, the judgment creditor must essentially sue again in order to enforce the hard-won judgment.

Real estate in the name of the judgment debtor can be seized, rented real estate or real estate titled in the name of a third party cannot. If you own an automobile it can be taken from you while a leased car cannot. A bank account in another state cannot be touched unless a procedure to domesticate the judgment is initiated in the new jurisdiction, and by then the debtor has wired out the money.

Hiding money in a foreign bank may discourage even the most aggressive creditor, who now has to retain a whole new set of attorneys and who will find that his previous attorneys are losing interest because their own national efforts have been exhausted.

The foreign attorneys will not take cases on contingency, or will speak of unfamiliar concepts such as "success fees," and will demand good money to be thrown at what may be bad, for the foreign bank account can easily be closed and the funds turned into third-party assets or wired to yet another jurisdiction, or "killed" through a disguised payment of another debt, leaving nothing to satisfy the judgment.

A person who is judgment-proof has no assets to satisfy any judgment entered against him. Because there is no debtor's prison, a person who is judgment-proof doesn't have to worry about paying a judgment and can even pretty much ignore legal proceedings filed against him.

It is common in divorce cases to see a husband with a six or seven-figure net worth—or even more—submit a financial affidavit claiming poverty shortly after the divorce papers are filed. His real money and assets are hidden.

The courts attempt to get around the concealment of wealth by imputing income. Unfortunately, few businesses will accept imputed dollars in exchange for services, and the poor wife who is stuck with imputed dollars had best leave her attorney behind in order to negotiate in good faith.

In many instances, lawyers will not even accept a case if they believe there are hidden assets or that enforcement of any judgment obtained will be problematic. As a face-saving measure, they will shift the discussion away from contingent fees and agree to commence representation on a profitable—that is, for the attorney—hourly basis. A plaintiff who believed essentially that he could get attorney services for "free"—but remember, nothing is free—on a contingent contractual basis never has the cash to hire that same worthy counsel on an hourly basis. And so the case is not pursued at all. Instead, the debtor, the contract breacher and the newly divorced have successfully followed the wise general Sun Tzu's advice and won the battle without ever engaging troops.

It is often said that "Possession is nine-tenths of the law." This is lawyer-speak. Ignore it. If you have something, it is yours. End of story.

Make it incredibly difficult for anyone to take your possessions away from you. If they don't know you own something, they can't come after it. That is the first rule.

If you leave the stolen painting on your wall, don't complain if a photographer taking a picture of your home for an unrelated purpose posts it in a public place where it can be seen and become the subject of replevin. Taking a selfie before such a painting, or with any of your other wealth is foolhardy. Flexing is stupid. Real wealth is always discreet.

Flexing is a great way to invite others to come and take away your wealth. Enjoy your wealth and your possessions discreetly. Let others believe in your enormous wealth and power; do not give them evidence to show that they are mistaken.

7

Love

LOVE AND FINANCE DON'T MIX. • TRUST IS THE BIGGEST LIABILITY OF ALL. • A LOVER IS A LUXURY, A SMART ACCOUNTANT IS A NECESSITY. • GOLD LASTS LONGER THAN LUST.

NEVER MIX LOVE AND MONEY. Spend your money on relationships if you want to, but do not mix the two. Doing so always ends in almost inconceivable anguish. A business partner may well betray you. That betrayal may bring a smirk to your face when you realize that you probably would have done the same, given the circumstances. But when a lover betrays you, anger can be uncontrollable. When a lover betrays you and takes your money, there can be no pardon. Relationships may come and go, but you can always use the money.

Love and materialism, the Chinese say, is just a pile of sand. Mixing business and romance is a deadly affair. Jealousy in one will spill over to the other with deadly effect. Your spouse knows where the bodies are buried, and while a good lawyer will take advantage of the taxman's "innocent spouse rule" do not believe that husbands and wives are ignorant of their partner's business affairs.

More likely than not, after a good score you boasted to your spouse how you beat someone in a transaction, how the dinner is paid for by a questionable tax deduction or cash income you didn't bother to declare. This kind of information is always of great interest to the authorities and they will be happy to grant immunity to anyone who accuses another of an unknown financial crime, whether married or otherwise.

The mere threat of exposure is enough to bend many a spouse to the will of another. Throw an aggressive family lawyer into the mix, the loss of a job—usually accompanying an aggressive, hostile divorce—and a bit of bad luck and then only disaster beckons.

Make payment a conscious choice. If you want to make gifts to a girlfriend, do so. But never go into business with a lover. Never combine business and pleasure. Never get into a relationship with a member of your staff. "When the fucking stops, the work stops," a wise business owner once said.

When the work stops, batten down the hatches and prepare for the inevitable sexual harassment lawsuit. No amount of lovey-dovey behavior will protect you from a former lover. Actions that you once thought romantic are now corrosive evidence of the charge. Both of you may have had different assumptions, different ideas about what would happen to the two of you in the future. Whatever these dreams were, they had no basis in reality. They were delusions, that is all.

No one will be sympathetic to your plight and juries love to punish. A broken love affair can mean loss of a job in addition to financial penalties. And if you are already married, add to the pain the costs of financing two divorce lawyers' extravagant lifestyles. In a divorce, if your partner knows your finances they will be in an excellent position to take them. They may simply seize your assets, whether you are entitled to them or not, with the understanding that a judge may in the future restore some of your wealth to you. But don't count on it. Most of this money will go to lawyers and the little that is left will not be enough to support you in the style you had become used to.

Pay your taxes, but by all means try to hide some cash. Secret stashes can come in handy when you are facing the street. A business negotiation—since, at the end of the day, that is what a divorce is—should not take place at knife point, while facing the threat of jail or garnishment of wages. Yet that is how these proceedings are routinely conducted.

Do not mix love and money. Love is not permanent. Love can be rented. Love that is purchased comes at a very high price.

8

Management

EMPLOYEES ARE THE RUNGS ON THE LADDER OF SUCCESS. DON'T HESITATE TO STEP ON THEM. • IT'S NEVER TOO LATE TO FIRE THE STAFF. • THE LESS EMPLOYEES KNOW ABOUT THE CASH FLOW, THE LESS THEY CAN DEMAND.

YOUR EMPLOYEES ARE neither your friends nor your family. They work for you. They are not your equals. If you have the power to fire them, don't be afraid to use it. There is usually a great deal of consternation when someone leaves. "Who will take care of Joe's work?" is heard more often than the sounds of mourning the recently fired.

The fact is that no one is irreplaceable. No one is essential. Few businesses collapse when an employee dies, no matter how well though-of, crucial or key he supposedly was to the business.

The Grammar of Money

As long as there are profits to be made, the business will go on.

One of the easiest ways to cut costs in a business is to fire employees. You can always cut staff. Fire one employee in a group of five and they will quickly adapt and regroup to cover the extra work—after all, that is what they do when someone goes on vacation. After a while, the extra work becomes the new normal. When the new normal becomes routine, fire another one. In most cases there will be no hit to production and the ones left will regroup and resort so as to take on the extra duties.

You cannot cut a group of three down anymore, because then you will no longer have a group, and two people who are resentful are difficult to control and may do a great deal of damage. The solution then is to consolidate departments while at the same time getting rid of an additional employee or two in the process. Before you know it you will have made substantial payroll cuts. These go directly to the bottom line, i.e., you own pocket.

As a general rule, a company can easily take a 10% reduction in force with no appreciable effect on production. The remaining employees will have to work harder, but so what? That is what they are paid to do.

CEO's who have won national reputations and obscene bonuses know this rule well. The remaining employees, fearful of losing their jobs, will do anything to keep theirs; they are happy to inform on their colleagues and identify the dead wood if they think that by doing so their own paychecks will keep on coming.

It is amazing that America is thought of as the land of opportunity while so many of its workers are terrified of losing their jobs. In other countries, when you are fired or laid off you go home, have a drink and start looking for a job. You still have your health care.

But not in the United States. The unemployment rate has been so high for so long and there is such a lack of jobs for minorities, older and younger workers that the callous treatment of employees means that when you are fired you go home and get a gun, come back and share your pain.

Some HR executives believe that it is best to pull the bandage off all at once rather than cutting slowly. Shock treatment may be a temptation, but it doesn't give the remaining–and perhaps soon to be laid off too–employees time to adapt, time to streamline. By the time they realize that the slow increase of temperature on the stove has reached a boil, they will be cooked. Slow, rolling layoffs are seldom even noticed, while shock treatment can even become news, causing your own customers to wonder what has happened as they look to your competitors.

The best destination for your non-performing employees is working for a competitor. This is a good way to discreetly damage a competitor's business while reducing your own costs.

Make a list of the dead wood and then praise them highly so that your competitor is anxious to bring them on board what will soon be his own sinking ship. Giving a lesser-performing employee an enthusiastic recommendation will lessen the pain of termination, especially if that employee finds a job with a competitor.

9

Misfortune

NEVER CONFUSE WEALTH WITH WISDOM. • WHEN LIFE HANDS YOU LEMONS, SELL THEM. • THEFT IS THE PENALTY FOR FAILURE TO DO DUE DILIGENCE. • THERE IS ALWAYS SOMEONE HAPPY TO TAKE YOUR MONEY. • TROUBLE COMES IN THREES.

NO MATTER WHAT YOU DO, misfortune will come your way. A wealthy businessman I know keeps what he calls a "consequences" file. For every time he is successful in a business deal and profits, someone, somehow materializes with a claim against the pot he has just filled with money. Whether a long written-off debt, an ex-spouse with a special need, an unbudgeted medical expense or a tax audit, there always appears an unexpected request for money.

You try to prepare for the unexpected as best you can, but the best preparation is to expect it.

If you know that it is going to happen at least you can be ready. Making the pot visibly smaller may be one way to deal with the problem, but there really is no universal solution to this particular problem.

Theodore Roosevelt once said, "For almost every gain there is a penalty." Someone will always appear who is more than happy to take your money. It is almost as if some quantum entanglement causes your money to cal out over dimensions announcing its presence and demanding others to come and take it away.

An ancient Arab proverb counsels "conceal thy travels and thy treasure." The reasons for this should be obvious: if you have accumulated wealth, it is at risk from those who learn of its existence. The warning against divulging your travel plans dates from the times when caravans criss-crossed Arabia and were at risk from armed marauders. These raiders were more than happy to fill their pockets with the booty stolen during a successful raid.

There are lessons for us even today. A newspaper reporter published an article about how an injured man had obtained a judgment against another driver for half a million dollars. The man's name was published, and that night his house was burglarized. The burglars figured either that the half million would be in the man's home. They were wrong, of course, money is not paid out in this fashion in tort cases.

Today one does not have to worry about marauding raiders, but burglars and thievery remain real problems. Whether you carry your wealth with you or not, remember that there is always someone ready to take it away.

Success does not necessarily lead to more success. Indeed, success may lead only to failure or oblivion. You may have just got a signing bonus, but if you use it to make a down payment on an expensive home, understand that there are no more signing bonuses coming and that if you live as if there were, you will lose that home.

Don't believe that just because you have once been successful that you will always be successful. More likely than not, your success was just a stroke of pure luck and won't happen again. What is much more likely is failure: a job you don't get, a raise beyond your reach, a bankrupt supplier, a jealous colleague and things turn to shit at once.

Keeping a little cash as an emergency fund is always a good idea, as is a bugout bag. A bugout bag is a packed suitcase you can pick up if you need to travel quickly. None of this, "I have to go home and pack." You're already packed. Keep a bugout bag in your home and another in your office. A third should be in the trunk of your car. When trouble comes, it may come hard and fast and you will be unable to negotiate when your normal surroundings become a battlefield. Trouble with the government is the worst of all but the easiest to negotiate from a distance.

For some reasons, trouble always comes in

threes. There never is just one problem. Sometimes the problems are connected even though the connection won't always be obvious. Marital problems can lead to poor performance at work. Money problems at work can lead to marital problems. Tax problems can trigger both. Illness can lead to a loss of work. In so many ways these issues are often connected. You cannot try to solve problems one at a time either, because they are connected. These problems may disappear, but usually they hang on and sometimes they hang on for years. It can take two years or more to get a tax problem resolved. Meanwhile, you don't have access to the cash. This causes your wife to think that you are a poor provider. Divorce proceedings follow and your wife's attorney believes, without evidence, that you are hiding money because "husbands always hide money." So he subpoenas your financial records from your place of employment. The bookkeeper sees this as additional work and moreover, wants no part of dealing with lawyers and subpoenas. So he passes it off to the firm's accountants, who charge not a small amount—including a look-see by their own attorneys—to put together a compliant answer to the subpoena. Who has to pay for this? You do. The firm deducts the full amount from your next paycheck, daring you to complain. This leaves less money to meet the outrageous temporary support order, a temporary state of affairs that serves only to put you under pressure while the case drags on—for at least a year and maybe two. You drink to forget and now you've got an alcohol problem. A DUI arrest is icing on the cake. At best all you can hope to do is stagger some of these matters. The DUI arrest left you with a suspended license, so you've got to wait that out. Maybe you could get a temporary transfer to some place where you do not need a car. The bills will pile up, but there is nothing you can do about that. Now you understand why all of a sudden the French Foreign Legion sounds like an attractive proposition.

You got into this mess because you let others take advantage of you. The only way out is take advantage of others. How you do this depends on the circumstances. Buy, beg, borrow or steal: the result is the same. It may be worth it to bite the bullet and pay more than what any problem is individually worth just to get out. Fighting problems, especially in court, is expensive. The justice system is outrageously expensive. Maybe you could beat the DUI charge but perhaps pleading guilty and taking the hit is the least expensive way to go. If you were in circumstances where all you had to deal with was one, single DUI, my advice might be to fight it. But fight a court case while surrounded by all sorts of other problems and distractions? You won't be able to do it. Take the hit and move on.

The same goes for the divorce. You were not put on this planet to fight this particular divorce case. No matter how much you think you love her, take the hit and move on. At work, if you can't mend fences, move on. Find another job. If you don't move on from misfortune you will have no chance of success, and if you have no chance of success you will not have any money to pay all these obligations anyway. Move on from misfortune, by all means necessary.

Losing a job is among the worst types of misfortune. Only when your income stops do you realize how much you depended on it. Often, the first inkling an employee gets of his termination is to find out that he is unable to log on to the network from his workdesk. Does anyone honestly think, in this day and age, that a corporation has any loyalty whatsoever to its employees? Of course not—that kind of reciprocal relationship was buried long ago. Corporations routinely let their employees go without any warning: indeed, IT departments cut off computer access as a prophylactic measure so that disgruntled employees are prevented from stealing confidential material or otherwise harming internal computer systems. This prevents the employee from copying that information necessary to protect himself from inquiries from third-party regulators. Since so many professions are regulated, lawyers, physicians, accountants, engineers— even hairdressers and barbers—this is a real problem. To protect yourself, make copies of key documents, by any means necessary. Once you lose access, you will not be able to.

Workplace obligations only run one way.

Even though a corporation will throw you out with no warning, they insist that you give at least two weeks' notice, and sometimes more, before leaving. There is no legal obligation requiring you to give any notice whatsoever. Threats to withhold paychecks or engage in other chickenshit behavior are hollow: the IRS will insist on the payment of its share and a call to them or the state's Department of Labor will usually move things along.

Never use the word "threat" under any circumstances. It is a federal felony to transmit a threat through the mail or Internet. Extortion is not an easy crime to defend. Instead, tell your employer that unless your check is delivered immediately that you will ask the assistance of a government agency in order to obtain compliance. Your employer will know what you mean. There is nothing in that request that is extortionate. A portion of your wages is due and owing to the Internal Revenue Service. Not only is your employer unjustifiably withholding your paycheck, they are unjustifiably retaining that portion owed to the IRS. The IRS moves quickly to resolve these 941 claims and will shut a business down if they think they are owed money.

10

Obligations

A DEAL IS A DEAL UNTIL A BETTER ONE COMES ALONG. • A CONTRACT IS NOT ALWAYS A CONTRACT. • CONTRACTS ARE WRITTEN ON SAND. • NO AGREEMENT IS BINDING. • BETRAY TO GET A BETTER DEAL.

CONTRACTS ARE WRITTEN ON SAND. The waves wash them away. At the commencement of a business relationship, both parties are happy. Both imagine that they will profit, and if we are being honest, each believes that he is taking advantage of the other, even in the most equal of circumstances. There is larceny in the hearts of both parties. Neither side feels that they have been particularly greedy and that their profit was reasonable under the circumstances.

It will come as a surprise to most people that contracts are not written in stone. Unlike the

Ten Commandments, contracts can and do change based on the circumstances of the parties. These occur at a personal as well as on a corporate level. A company that is cannot or simply does not want to meet its obligations will file for bankruptcy to get out of them. Wall Street teasingly calls this a "haircut," but no one is laughing when the bill collector knocks at your door. What's good for the goose is good for the gander: you can file for bankruptcy as well. Or you can simply threaten to file in order to rewrite the contract. No one wants to be an unsecured creditor in a bankruptcy. You get nothing. Half the time it's not even worth the legal fees to file a claim. Ah, you say, but a secured creditor can repossess your vehicle.

Let him. You're probably upside down in the car anyway, a victim of seven year loans and easy financing. It's not all that easy to get rid of a car when you owe more than what the car is worth. So let the creditor—who isn't even the dealer anyway, it's an impersonal paperholder because the loan has already been sliced and diced and securitized— and who doesn't want to spend money to pay a repo man to go out and pick up the car. That will be an additional unwanted expense.

Creditors will do nearly anything to keep the cash flow coming, and all you want, after all, is for them to take a bit of a haircut. You'll make payments at a lower rate. And then they don't have to spend money repo'ing a car that will be difficult to sell.

Sometimes, creditors play tough don't work debts out until there's a parking lot full of cars and their cash flow is impaired. Then someone —hopefully wiser—will step in and try to work out the problem debts. These debts could have been worked out long ago with a reasonable discount and lower monthly payments.

It is not easy to get the attention of these wise men, and sometimes all you can do to make them understand you are serious is to default. That will get their attention. Your credit rating will take a hit, but it will take a hit anyway because you can't make the payments. Don't worry too much, there are millions whose credit reports turned to crud after foreclosures and the financial crisis of 2008-2009, but so much of that negative information comes off after seven years. Even bankruptcies only stay on for ten. There are many waiting patiently for a bankruptcy to drop off their credit report. Though the federal government never throws away court records, it will be very difficult to uncover whether an individual filed for bankruptcy once the bankruptcy is removed from the credit report and a sufficiently long period has passed. Time here does what God cannot, that is, change the past.

Judgments stay on longer; a judgment can be collected for a period of twenty years. And though judgments can be enforced for twenty years, trying to enforce a two-decades old order is no trivial matter. After such a long period of time, few even will recall the precise circumstances that gave rise to the debt. Decades old debt is written off and forgotten.

The only true constant is change. Circumstances change, seemingly all at once. Market prices, thought to be stable fall precipitously due to a black swan event. No one imagined that things could ever be this bad. Your counterparty, sits gloating. His profits have increased a thousand-fold; he smiles as he reminds you of your duty of performance under the contract.

In international business, contracts are documents that routinely reach 25 pages or more in length for even minor matters, and for large projects, a two or three hundred page contract with annexes and assurances and side letters is not uncommon.

Except in China. Even today, a Chinese contract is often just one or two pages long. This is not because the Chinese do not intend to perform the contract, they do. They fully intend to meet those obligations undertaken at the time of the signing of the contract. But Chinese business, unlike business in the West, views contracts as malleable because circumstances change.

What we agree upon today can and will be affected by what happens tomorrow. It is naive to believe that a contract can anticipate each and every contingency, occurrence or event that might affect the parties down the road and cause them to back away from their obligations. Americans call this a breach of contract. The Chinese call this a change of circumstances.

There are many terms which describe what happens to the parties when they seek to alter their agreements based on changed circumstances. Some might call it a restructuring; others a novation. Both describe a new beginning, a changed relationship between the parties due to circumstances that changed, even if only one side anticipated the change.

If you are in the position of the gloating counter-party, of course you scream and shout at even the suggestion that the contracts be rewritten and insist on full and complete compliance. Nothing short of full compliance is satisfactory. But if you are on the potentially losing side, you have to ignore the contract, beg for a restructuring, and if all your counter-party can do is gloat, tell him to fuck off, that you have no intention of performing under the changed circumstances.

Soon his gloating will turn to terror because if he goes to the marketplace he will find that prices there have increased dramatically—due to the change of circumstances—and it isn't that easy to find someone willing to perform at all. So after a while he comes back and agrees to a restructuring.

But now, emboldened, you ask for more. You claim that the depth of the change is more than you had anticipated earlier. If he sues you it will be years before he can get a judgment, and by then the commercial situation may have improved. If you are smart, you are judgment-proof anyway, doing business through an asset-less shell. Commercial arbitration is attractive but only works if the parties in good faith appear before the arbitral tribunal. Otherwise it is worse, just as expensive as litigation and you still end up in court.

It should be obvious that you should only adhere to any commitment you have made unless a better deal comes along. Claim the new deal as your own and jettison the old. Will you get sued? Maybe. When you have a certain amount of money, you realize that litigation is a cost of doing business. But most are so afraid of the cost that they let matters slide and never appear in court. This is true even amongst the largest corporations. Often a strongly-worded letter will do the trick and send a plaintiff on his way. But never assume that this tactic will work.

No agreement is written in stone. Any contract can be modified. Do not be afraid to change circumstances on paper to match the reality of changed circumstances.

11

Profit

THERE ARE MANY PATHS TO MONEY. • SOMETIMES THE QUICKEST WAY TO FIND PROFITS IS TO LET THEM FIND YOU. • TAKE JOY FROM PROFIT. • EVEN IN THE WORST OF TIMES SOMEONE TURNS A PROFIT. • PROFIT IS ITS OWN JUSTIFICATION. • NEVER ALLOW DOUBT TO SLOW YOUR PURSUIT OF PROFIT. • OPPORTUNITY PLUS INSTINCT EQUALS PROFIT. • FLATTERY IS NECESSARY FOR SUCCESS. • WAR IS GOOD FOR BUSINESS. PEACE IS GOOD FOR BUSINESS. • THE EARLY INVESTOR REAPS THE MOST INTEREST. • PROFIT TRUMPS EMOTION. • KNOWLEDGE EQUALS PROFIT.

GREED IS the only way to success, but there are many paths to profit. Just because you do not know which road is right for you today doesn't mean that road does not exist at all. Surely it does. It is just a question of finding it, of applying creativity to a fixed set of circumstances. If the circumstances prevent your personal enrichment, change them. Move to another place, another country, anywhere you can profit. If you cannot see a way to move, by all means stay in your place and take advantage of the people around you. Find ways to put their money into your pocket, by buying and selling, charging a commission or providing a service. Steal a better job. Always put yourself over everybody else. In the long run, this is survival.

Do not expect anyone to show you the way, either. A physician can do his part to save the world but real money is made performing cosmetic surgery for the wealthy trying to stave off the calendar. Success isn't measured in the god business by piety, but how much cash comes in on the collection plate. Paying for heating or cooling those mega-churches ain't cheap. You certainly have heard of the "lawsuit lottery." In the United States at least, for many the law business is personal injury business. If you knew that you were going to law school and would spend the rest of your life prosecuting or defending personal injury actions, you would have paid a little more attention in your STEM classes.

Land was traditionally a path to profit. People believe that fee simple ownership of land is a guaranteed path to profit.

A studio condo in an only OK building is not the same as a producing soybean farm, yet people who purchase such condos imagine themselves to be rentier landlords. 2008 teaches that real estate prices can go down. What keeps them up is that everyone thinks they can make a killing. Television shows preach the gospel of flipping real estate. Anyone can become wealthy by flipping, they claim. Even celebrities famous for only being famous imagine themselves businessmen because they have bought a property, made cosmetic improvements, and then sold it to someone else. The leader of the country was a real estate developer, after all.

Making something new where there was nothing before is really the only way to create real value. In every other endeavor, you are only a parasite. Developers who construct buildings are in one class, the studio condo buyer another. So much manufacturing has moved to China, but manufacturing remains one of the best paths to profit. Unfortunately, it is out of the reach of most people.

It is impossible to tell which or what kind of business will be successful. Once, there were 10,000 specialty camera stores in the United States. A camera manufacturer was assured of 20,000 sales whenever a new model was introduced because each store would buy at least two copies. Only 500 or so stores remain and the manufacturers know that Amazon isn't buying that many cameras.

Once upon a time the only way to buy an airplane ticket, was directly from the airline or through travel agents. There were thousands of travel agents throughout the country. The few that survive do so by selling cruises. Many will no longer even bother to sell airline tickets because the margins are so thin. What was once a sinecure barely survives. Record stores have mostly disappeared, bookstores will be next. Do not think that the newest and coolest technologies are safe either. In the past few years, thousands of vaping shops magically appeared; now, just like Internet cafes, whose numbers were once legion, they are all, one by one, shutting down. Deaths linked to vaping certainly didn't help, but there were no such highly-publicized tragedies that decimated the Internet cafe business: the kinks were worked out of wireless and home Internet access became ubiquitous.

Only one thing is for sure: if you find a profitable niche, don't wait for it to become unprofitable. Drop it, sell it to someone else and get out before the collapse.

12

Real Property

THE AMERICAN DREAM HAS A USEFUL LIFE. • REAL ESTATE IS NEVER MORE THAN AN ASSET. • THE "FOR SALE" SIGN STAYS UP AFTER CLOSING. • BEWARE OF THOSE CHARGING COMMISSIONS. • APPRAISALS ARE ASTROLOGY. • STAGING IS A NECESSARY SKILL FOR ALL INTERACTIONS. • LOCATION, LOCATION, LOCATION.

THE "AMERICAN DREAM" is an owner-occupied, single family home. What people forget is that real estate is a depreciating asset. What kind of a "dream" depreciates over time?

Real estate is only profitable if you own multiple properties. The need for a place to sleep is biological. Yet as Robert Kiyosaki pointed out in *Rich Dad, Poor Dad*, not only is the family home a depreciating asset, it is an asset which produces no income and in all cases a money pit taking money out of your pocket where it belongs.

Some will argue that real estate always appreciates. This was disproved in the crash of 2009 where appraised equity simply disappeared. Ten years later, real estate prices haven't exactly recovered either. But let's assume for a moment that there was no crash and you were successful in taking out your equity. You still need a place to sleep. Unless you're happy sleeping in your car—illegal in the City of Los Angeles, by the way—you have to purchase another property. Do you think that somehow, magically, the price of that property hasn't similarly increased? If you want to speculate, that is, invest in real estate, feel free to do so as long as you have found a place to stay. These days renting is probably a better value proposition, but this depends on the neighborhood and many other variables.

In the United States, at least, holding on to real estate is expensive. Property taxes rise each year and eat away a little more of your holdings. Condominium association fees these days cost as much as a mortgage. If you are on a fixed income—or if you have lost your job—a calculator will tell you how long you have before your property is taken away from you. This is one of the reasons why wealth rarely lasts for more than three generations.

The taxes on a million dollar home are eye-watering. And if you live in your home the only tax break is the ever-decreasing interest deduction. Of course, if you have no income the deductions are irrelevant, useless and lost. The reality is that from time to time, you will have no income. Unless you can pay cash for real estate, you own nothing. You are servicing debt, and in exchange for this debt service you get to gamble that your asset will appreciate and meanwhile, you have a place to sleep.

Don't even use the word "home," it is just too loaded with unproductive baggage. That piece of real estate your children and wife love is just another asset. As mentioned in other places in this book, keep the "for sale" sign up and be ready to sell quickly. Never become emotionally attached to any asset.

Don't get caught up in believing that the family home is ever anything more than simply another asset. It is a deadly mistake to attach sentimental value to any of your assets. Everything you own should always be for sale, whenever you can make a profit. Real estate agents make a point of taking down the "For Sale" sign immediately upon closing a purchase contract. Don't be fooled—the sign stays up, but at an increased price. If you can make $50,000 on the transaction, you can sell the next day. Other homes in the neighborhood, the famous "comparables" will not increase in value so quickly. But wait—they just might, because you have made the sale.

Someone may come along, a true "motivated

buyer" who really needs your property. If you can put substantial cash in your pocket, let him have it. Your second choice, the property you were going to buy, or even your third choice, is still on the market. The seller will be happy you came back, you can still negotiate his selling price down and it is easier to do so with an extra fifty-thousand in your pocket. The real estate agent will, of course, complain that it's a bad idea to keep the "For Sale" sign up, but remind the agent that if he wants to earn his commission he's got a limited time to do so.

Real estate salespeople are pitiless—they understand that real estate is merely a commodity like any other. If they can turn around and sell your property the next day for an inflated price the comparables must somehow have been wrong.

As a general rule, though, it is a good idea not to trust anyone whose involvement in the deal revolves around their ability to charge a commission. In addition to real estate brokers, plaintiff personal injury attorneys, "finder's fee" operators, there are many, many who bring little real value to the table. Because there is no reality to their services, they can and do argue with their colleagues about who properly has "earned" a fee—that is, after doing little other than refer a matter out—and insist upon its payment—from your money, of course.

Multi-million dollar businesses have been based on "cutting out the middleman" so the idea of eliminating those who would seek a commission is hardly a novel one. The individual who charges a commission for his services has no loyalty to you, his loyalty is only to that commission. This is different from a person who sells, that is, parts with a product. If you do not buy, he can sell to someone else. There is always a customer for everything. But a commission-seeker relies not on his own asset, but on yours. In a real sense, someone who charges a commission is your partner, whether you consider him your partner or not. But this partner's interest is not the same as yours. Do not ever forget this.

How much is your home worth? The principal way to determine the value of an unsold home is through a real estate appraisal. Appraisers charge north of $500—sometimes much more—to drive around a neighborhood and take a look at your home before coming up with a report that justifies a number that often is pulled out of thin air.

Don't obsess about whether a bedroom needs a new coat of paint, or whether you should have a finished basement. The appraiser won't even come into your home. He couldn't care less. He will look at recent sales, add a factor for how much homes are appreciating generally—or not—in your city, throw in a fudge factor, pull up a template, and voila—you have an estimate of value. Such an estimate is worth little more than voodoo, a crystal ball or tarot cards. It would be interesting to compare the accuracy of appraisals to actual home sale prices, but this is like asking a surgeon how many of his patients died on the operating table. You won't find appraisers boasting that their appraisals are 90% accurate for the simple reason that they are not.

Appraisals are astrology, wishful thinking, optimistic hopes. Don't put your trust in them. And don't worry about appraisers actually coming inside your home. They don't need to and they don't want to waste their time listening to you blab on about how you in fact repainted one of the bedrooms and how nice it looks. They don't care. There is no need to stay home for the appraiser. You don't have to. You won't even know when he drove past your house in the neighborhood because the only reason to drive past is to make sure that the structure is still standing.

When the same appraiser needs to play down the value of a home for say, a divorce proceeding, the number he comes up with would make you wonder why the same home that was appraised at nearly a million dollars was now priced at little more than tear-down value. This is because the appraisal conforms to fit the narrative told by the person paying the appraiser. The same house appraised for a loan will have an exaggerated value.

"Staging" refers to renting expensive furnishings in order to make a house more attractive. In other words, staging is the use of deception to entice a buyer to make a purchase. Expensive furniture, far beyond what you would ever buy, can be rented for an open house. Lavish furnishings will make an ordinary home look like it might even be worth the exaggerated appraisal.

The minute the open house is finished the lavish furnishings will be carted away, and the day to day accumulation of dirt will begin again. Your house was never as clean as before a staged open house, nor will it ever be again. The idea is to delude potential buyers that this is what their new home will look like on a day to day basis. This won't be true unless they arrange for the purchase of similar lavish furnishings and scrub the home on a daily basis.

A staging is a play, a make-believe that has little connection with reality. When you go to the theater, you know that the actors are playing roles and that none of it is real. Buyers make the mistake of failing to realize that when they visit a staged home, they are in a theater as well, with curated furnishings carefully stage managed. The play's director is the almost too-friendly real estate agent.

Why do you think that the real estate agent does not want you anywhere near this carefully choreographed presentation? Because you might interrupt the programmed showing with the truth. A look of surprise when the agent boasts of how wonderful the local schools are might suggest to a buyer that it is the first time you have heard anyone say such things about that local school with the drugs and gang problems.

The real estate agent is an experienced actor who knows what to say and when to cut to a commercial.

Learn from these actors. "Staging" should be a part of your everyday business life. All business interactions can be and should be staged. Sell the optimism, sell the dream, but make the sale. There are many realities. Your interest as seller is different from the seller's interest and the real estate agent has his own agenda. Every transaction of any kind can be stage managed. Do so, if you want to be successful. Have you ever heard of a real estate agent being criticized for painting a too-rosy picture of a home?

13

Religion

THE GOD BUSINESS IS A BUSINESS LIKE ANY OTHER. • SOME PEOPLE DOUBT THE EXISTENCE OF GOD, BUT NO ONE DOUBTS THE EXISTENCE OF MONEY. • ONLY THE RICH CAN GIVE TO THE POOR. • GOD CANNOT SPEND MONEY.

RELIGIONS TEACH the value of giving alms to the poor, but the passed collection plate is not for the disadvantaged, it is for the church itself. Whether donations are made on a weekly, pray as you go basis, or annually, buying seats for the High Holy Days, or even government-funded as in Germany and Saudi Arabia, churches are businesses like any other. In order to pray, the faithful must pay. It is just that simple.

St. Francis of Assisi is one of the great holy men of the Roman Catholic Church. He lived a life of extreme, exemplary poverty. Looked at in another way, he was an itinerant tramp who moved from town to town on the bum freeloading off of the people he met or the monasteries he visited.

A religion that sets up a homeless tramp as a paragon to virtue can only do so when backed by centuries of great wealth, secret banks and extensive multi-national real estate holdings.

Catholic priests take no vow of poverty. That in itself should tell you something. Then there is the prosperity gospel preached by ministers like Johnny Dollar and Joel Osteen. These churches include God in their theology of greed. If God helps you to get rich by all means put him on your team. But keep any money destined for the deity in your own pocket. He can't spend it anyway.

Look at religion: educated people can only believe because they were indoctrinated at an early age. Every single religion is full of absurdities. The great doctor of the Church, Tertullian, even admitted, "I believe because it is absurd."

Take advantage of the credulity of others. If someone is foolish enough to believe that Joseph Smith translated the Book of Mormon from gold plates in an unknown language which were subsequently hidden in New York by an angel, they might well believe your story about—well, anything: why you were late for work, why they should buy your product, why there is a lifetime warranty, why whatever. Always take advantage of their credulity.

The Talmud suggests that the Virgin Mary had an affair with a Roman soldier and fell pregnant. The New Testament teaches that God himself inseminated her, while preserving her virginity. Which is easier to believe? In *One Hundred Years of Solitude*, Gabriel Garcia Marquez tells of a young woman who was so beautiful that she ascended into heaven. That at least, was the story her embarrassed parents told in order to hide the inconvenient truth that she ran away with a traveling salesman.

You are free to believe whatever truths comfort you. Religion, on the whole, brings good things to society. A wise imam once said, "if they're praying five times a day, at least then they're not out committing crimes." If others seek comfort in faith, let them do so. But do not believe that there is any truth except your own.

The only virtue in the religion of money is greed.

If you want a way to combine religion and commerce, consider getting a job with an NGO, a church, or some institution dedicated to the poor. There are many. The pay is low, but it's still cash. John D. Rockefeller said that the power to make money is a gift from God. Let Jesus put money into your pocket.

14

Risk and Reward

RISK DOESN'T ALWAYS EQUAL REWARD. • GREAT RISK MAY BRING GREAT PROFIT. • SMALL PRINT LEADS TO LARGE RISK. • DANGER AWAITS WHEN THINGS GO WELL.

FAILURE IS EVERYWHERE. Hard work is no guarantee of success, but little work guarantees failure. The one wild card is luck. Luck, or fate, destiny, or fortune cannot be controlled. Luck either is there or it is not there. You cannot change your luck. You can maneuver yourself into a position where if luck strikes you will more likely be able to take advantage of it but you cannot control whether luck will come or not. There are simply too many variables. If you never sit down at a casino, you will never be able to win a jackpot.

In their song, *Uncle John's Band,* The Greatful

Dead warned, "when life looks like Easy Street, there is danger at your door." Danger awaits the successful. For each success, prepare for catastrophe. Do not think that success follows catastrophe. It is much more likely that catastrophe will be followed by more woe.

An aircraft mechanic once dreamt of becoming a pilot but he could never make the grade. He got an air transport license so he could move airplanes on the tarmac—management would never let him get in the air. Still, he had the license, a license obtained by diligent effort over nights and weekends. Then, one day, his airline merged with another and since his name was on the list of license-holders, he gained a low-rung seniority position with the new airline with almost no flight experience.

This was in the days of the B-727, an airplane that required three licensed pilots, one of whom was the flight engineer whose job it was to monitor systems. He only bid on flights where he could "fly the board" and started earning a salary that real pilots earned. His friends kept him away from the left seat, and he was happy.

The pilot's salary that he earned thanks to the merger and a union contract never would have happened were it not for the luck of an airline merger. He could just as easily have been let go, which is what usually happens in a merger. By hard work he put himself in a position to take advantage were luck to come along. And finally, he was smart enough not to demand too much, lest he be sent back to the ground as an airline mechanic.

You cannot plan for circumstances like these. They are rare and rarely repeat. Airline mergers still take place, new airlines are formed all the time; the 727 no longer flies regularly and the standard pilot complement in a modern airliner is two, not three. But that does not mean you can no longer find analogous opportunities. Always be on the lookout to step up on the ladder, even if to reach the next rung you have to step on the hands of those you would leave below.

Successful investments are all too often the function of luck. The WeWork example shows that even companies valued at 47 billion dollars by Wall Street can blow up when the public realizes that the emperor wears no clothes. Even Goldman took a hit on its investment, which shows that delusions run deep on Wall Street. Great risk does not bring great reward, it only puts you in a position that is even more precarious. Crime carries risk—sometimes great risk—and the rewards are usually insubstantial.

In business lawyers hope to trick their clients' counterparties by burying risk in small print. They mumble something about "using the form" and hope that no one bothers to read the form's onerous provisions. Because the form is printed, businessmen all too often are deluded into thinking that the form can't be changed. In the days the laser printer, "printed" means using a sans-serif font instead of Times Roman.

Keep in mind that the form came off the screen and through the laser printer before it is put in front of you to sign. Feel free to cross-out any provisions that are onerous or that you don't understand. Making corrections is a trivial case of going back to the keyboard and a few clicks. You can always vary the terms of any printed contracted before you sign it.

There are legal defenses to small print but there is no point to going over them here. It is usually enough to say that you did not agree to these provisions. Unless your counter-party is a bank or a government, there will be complaints, denials and squawking. Ignore the noise. A contract can be rewritten. Trickster small print should not be given effect unless the parties agree to it, and in any case should not last forever.

More often than not, risk is only risk and brings no reward whatsoever. Do not think that because you have risked anything that you will be entitled to a reward. If anything, the converse is true: risk all and receive no reward.

IN ANY HUMAN INTERACTION, try to determine how you can benefit. If there is no benefit, why are you engaging in the transaction? Profit comes quickly or not at all. Delayed profit is faith, a belief in a deity who does not believe in you. Maybe circumstances will be remain constant and promises to pay, or share in fees will be honored. But more likely than not, the circumstances will have changed, or your counter-party will claim that they have changed, and will use this "fact" to whine and complain and deny paying you your share. If you cannot profit in the short term, walk away.

Banks used to service long term mortgages, making money over the years as homeowners slowly paid down their notes. But now a bank will sell the mortgage it has written at an immediate discount and pocket its profits immediately. Collection and servicing the mortgage are now the problem of the buyer of the mortgage, who securitizes it and outsources these tasks to someone else. The bank is out of the loop and no longer even pretends to care about its borrower one way or the other.

Meanwhile, a smart buyer has put the house back on the market in hopes of flipping it to a motivated buyer who needs a place to sleep—maybe one of the newly divorced—and will happily sign over the mortgage to the new buyer, who never even met the bank's loan officers.

The paper takes on a life of its own, because by now it has been securitized. The anonymization of these transactions, removing the human element makes default a smart business move if prices drop or if whoever holds the obligation under the paper loses a job or is laid off.

Everyone involved is chasing the quick buck. No one cares about you, so why should you care about them? Look out for yourself. No one else will.

GETTING a bad deal is usually the result of a failure to do due diligence, an awkward phrase used in the financial world that means "to investigate." That is, to take the claims made and the assertions written by a counter-party and try to verify them, not through the counter-party's own sources of information, but fact-checking as would any responsible journalist. Like a tax audit, it means not taking any assertion on good faith and instead demanding strict proof. If a company claims that it grossed 4 million dollars last year, you want to see the bank deposits. And not photocopies of the deposits unless the bank itself is directly providing them to you. Forging documents today is trivial and unless you get caught in a lame error—like Dan Rather's staffers who were unfamiliar with font-sets in the days of the typewriter—it is difficult to get caught out.

Madoff forged trading records for years and no one noticed. The SEC let him slide because it failed to do a thorough investigation. The SEC was lulled into complacency because the idea that a former head of NASDAQ and a respected trader on the Street was running a Ponzi scheme was preposterous. Never mind that no one ever seemed to trade with Madoff and his famous reliable split/strike conversions. The obvious answer, that no one was trading with Madoff meant that Madoff wasn't trading, was conveniently forgotten. Madoff got lucky. A more in-depth analysis would have revealed Madoff's Ponzi scheme.

The fact that no one could find a trader on Wall Street who traded with billionaire Jeffrey Epstein suggests that Jeffrey Epstein was not trading. The questions surrounding his supposed suicide while in a high-security federal prison put an end to the investigation of the sources of Jeffrey Epstein's wealth because it was much more interesting to speculate on whether or not he killed himself. The sources of Epstein's wealth were lost in the speculation as to who might have had Epstein murdered.

In all these cases, a more in-depth investigation would have revealed the real facts at issue, the nature of the money flow.

In a proper due diligence exercise, a team of accountants and investigators will look at everything. Every little thing. The danger is that when they can''t find anything and nevertheless believe that something is there, that they will make up facts. Donald Trump must have been up to no good on his pre-presidential trips to Russia, hence the gossip-filled Steele Dossier. If facts cannot be corroborated, they are not facts. They are opinions and articles of faith.

Do not enter into any transaction armed with only uncorroborated facts unless you don't care if you lose in the transaction. And if you don't care, why are you engaging in the first place? Time constraints may prevent you from conducting a full in-depth due diligence investigation, but be aware that any potential problems are hiding wherever you were unable to investigate prior to closing the deal. Continue to focus your attention on these areas more than any other, because that's where the surprises are waiting.

When someone says, "take my word for it," don't. Say, we couldn't corroborate x or y, so we'll need a discount to cover contingencies. No discount and an insistence that there's nothing really to investigate? Walk away. Few were brave enough to walk away from Madoff, but many did. You want to be one of those who left the magical profits on the table because they weren't magical at all. They were instead the records of multiple thefts and crimes.

15

Self-Interest

ALWAYS ASK, "WHAT'S IN IT FOR ME?" • ALWAYS ASK, "AM I GOING TO GET PAID FOR THIS?" • GOOD DEEDS ARE SELDOM PROFITABLE. • THERE'S NOTHING WRONG WITH CHARITY AS LONG AS IT WINDS UP IN YOUR POCKET. • THERE IS NO SUCCESS WITHOUT BETRAYAL. • IDENTIFY THE ENEMY

ACCORDING to Ming Dynasty official Li Zongwu, writing in the early 20TH century, the only path to success is through unrestrained selfishness. You must put your own interests above those of all others. If you do not benefit from an activity do not engage in it. If there is no profit, the activity is not worthwhile.

By refusing to perform tasks sought to be imposed by others, refusing to participate or take on a task can free up enormous amounts of time. The way importance is measured in society is through money. Money is the way of keeping score. If it's not important enough for them to pay you, it's not important enough for you to lift a finger. People should know that if they want you to participate—in anything—your participation doesn't come free. No cash, no honoraria or no paycheck means that the matter at hand isn't important enough to the person trying to get you involved. So why should you?

Charity and alms-giving should be your own personal choice. Don't get involved unless you can profit personally, such as by getting a board membership, club membership or some other perk you normally wouldn't be entitled to. You cannot save the poor. Once you realize this, any residual guilt you had about them will fade away. There have always been poor people. There will always be poor people. There will be people who simply do not understand money. In your fleeting time on the planet, there is little you can do to improve the plight of the impoverished. So don't even waste your time trying, unless you enjoy trying to save the people and the planet. In that sense, for you, trying to save the poor is entertainment.

LOOKING out for yourself is crucial for the simple reason that no one else will look out for you. There is all sorts of palaver in business about finding a mentor who can help you navigate through the company and who can help your career, but this is all nonsense. The mentor is looking out for his own interests. At a basic level he wants someone to do his work, or who will be on a team that he is responsible for that is lacking in expertise or workers. You are helping him just as much as he is helping you.

Do not think that the—as opposed to 'your'—mentor is doing you any favors. He didn't get to be where he is in the organization through altruism and charitable works. He got there through the dark arts of this *Grammar*, the *Art of War* and Thick Black theory. The truth is that you are doing him a favor, and do not ever let him forget it. Everything should be on a quid pro quo basis.

At some point, your mentor may ask you to do something illegal. Think long and hard before you agree. By illegal I do not merely refer to the violation of a statute, but also the breaking of any internal rule of the company. The minute you agree, whether you do what he asks or not, you are in his power.

The crime of "conspiracy" is the crime of agreement. You can still be guilty of a conspiracy if all you do is agree and other than nod your head, you never did anything else. The law is strange in that way, a relic of medieval English palace intrigues. The minute you agree he has something over you. You may think you have something on him, but his higher position in the organization means that his colleagues will come to his aid. No one will come to yours. Better not to agree at all. Act offended and find another mentor. Leak vague reasons why this was necessary. Others will figure it out and probably suspect worse.

The mentor/mentee relationship is similar to the dynamic between employers and job-seekers. The job seeker puts up his hand and begs, "please pick me," not realizing that the employer is desperate to fill a slot. Rebecca didn't come into work today, who will pick up her files? Better get someone in here quick. The person who suffers in these circumstances is Rebecca's supervisor, the one who has the responsibility of making sure that Rebecca's work gets done, not someone in the HR department, whose responsibility, it would seem, is to make sure that incoming resumes usually find their way into the trash.

It is easy to say, "look out for yourself" but it is not always easy to put the principle into practice amidst a crowd of beggars, influence-seekers and others looking out for themselves and immediate gratification. The solution, the god people would say, is to love one another. Nonsense. There will always be those in the group who will take advantage of his fellow man no matter what. Turning the other cheek means only that it is more likely that they will land a punch on that cheek too.

You have to be better than that, you have to be more adept at taking advantage. Never let anyone else take advantage of you. Ignore requests that come from the disadvantaged.

Make time for your profit-seeking adventures by saying "no" to everyone else's "yes," unless there is a substantial chance for your own profitable participation. If you are not paid up-front, take a post-dated check, stock certificates, anything in writing that can be used later on. If someone else says, "don't worry about it, we'll take care of it later on," it means that they only will take care of themselves. Your money and your right to it will soon be quickly forgotten. This acutely applies to freelancers. They will try to pay freelancers with pablum like, "we thought you were doing this for the exposure," or, "paid work will come from this," or even, "we promise to roll you over onto the next project."

Never believe them. Say "no." If they need you badly enough they will pay, and if they do not pay you do not need them. The worst thing is having to neglect your lucrative, paying work to finish jobs you promised to perform for no money at all.

What to do? The answer is simple: drop out of the non-paying jobs. There will be great weeping and gnashing of teeth with efforts to shame you into continuing. You promised. You said you'd have this for our March issue. Now what are we going to do? Ignore them. Tell them you have to focus on your paying clients and not your charity clients. They will hate this term and loudly protest that they are not a charity. You feign confusion, and mention how poor they said they were and how that was the reason why they couldn't pay your normal rate. Their protests will soon turn to threats. Notice, though, how no one is even remotely concerned about your issues, your problems, your bills, your own need for money. It is all about them.

If you don't perform you'll be blacklisted. You'll never work for us again (ironic, since you're not working for them in the first place). We'll tell others what you did, how you left us in the lurch. Ignore each and every one of these useless, meaningless empty threats. Simply reiterate that you cannot afford to do charity work any longer. If they want you to finish the project they will have to pay, and not at the end of the project. The things they said, the threats they made have caused you to lose trust. There will have to be a substantial advance because you no longer believe that they would ever pay you in the future.

This can go two ways, but either way you win. First, you get out of completing your charity project. Second, you get paid for it. The second alternative is by far the better one, but it's not so bad if you make more time available by dropping the non-paying project. Let them moan and scream, they can do nothing. Sue you for breach of contract? Not so fast. They weren't paying you, so under American law there is no consideration for the contract, meaning it is voidable at any time. Were you to drop dead they would manage. So they will manage without you as well. After all, if they are not paying, you really were never part of the team. You were just someone they could take advantage of.

WHENEVER YOU FIND yourself in a new position, immediately try to identify your enemy. There will alway be one. Always. There is someone trying to manipulate the boss from behind the curtain, someone trying to blame his own failures on you. You are, after all, the new guy, the new kid on the block. You are vulnerable. Your enemy will try to find any black marks in your background, any holes, and bring them to the fore. Prior failings will be researched and you need to have answers, a cover story, a way to protect yourself. Do not be surprised if decades-old matters are unearthed and discussed as if they occurred yesterday.

Your advantage is that you know what really happened and so can seed your lies with the truth. When accused, use a few indisputable but forgotten facts to weave a tale that makes you the hero, even to cover up a disaster. You went to prison to protect someone else. You couldn't tell the truth then because if you did hundreds would have lost their jobs. You remember the incident as having taught you the value of loyalty.

In this fashion, you can mitigate the harm that will be caused by your enemies. And when your boss asks you about these events, tell him that you did not want to boast about what others consider shameful—because for you, these events were a badge of honor. Your boss will be pleased.

Tactical denial is a short-term strategy. Refuse to engage. There will always be some doubt, and time erases the details of events. Maybe you honorably took the fall for someone else. The boss will be pleased to learn that you were loyal even at the risk of personal career disaster. It is a lot easier to spin a story when details are forgotten and nowhere is there to correct you.

16

Strategy and Tactics

Keep your eyes open. • Hide your travels and your treasure. • Choose no side but your own. • Never admit anything; always blame others. • Expand or die. • Better to ask for forgiveness than permission. • Never ask when you can take. • Always urge others to volunteer. • Never get into anything that you can't get out of. • Never rush to pay a debt. • Always leave yourself an out. • Buy when everyone else is selling and hold until everyone else is buying. • Wait to bid until your opponents have exhausted themselves. • Promise everything, deliver nothing.

NAPOLEON SAID, "to be a success in this world, promise everything, deliver nothing." To keep your money, there are general rules of behavior you must follow. The most important aspect of strategy and tactics is to realize that they are needed at all. These are, after all, tools necessary to implement acts of war. The sooner you realize that you are in a war, the war for money and profit, the better off you will be.

Be observant. Awareness of your surroundings and the general situation is crucial. Urge others to volunteer. You should not be seen as shirking a duty, but neither should you undertake obligations that will bring no reward. Paying a debt at the last minute not only gives you the use of someone else's money for as long a time as possible, but circumstances may change so as to erase the debt. Your creditor may go bankrupt and the trustee decides it's not worth the trouble to pursue unsecured debts. Your creditor dies without having formally memorialized the debt. Upon the death of a debtor, credit card companies routinely write off debt rather than spend money on attorneys to file a claim in probate for an estate that may have no assets and may never be opened. They do not want to incur attorneys fees chasing money that will never be repaid.

Beware of admissions. Admitting to an adverse position, confessing to a wrong or even a debt will only serve to assist those who seek to take money out of your pocket. Agree only to pay judgments properly won, and then only after asking the court for a payment plan. Payment plans are almost always given and the creditor may well abandon the suit because he has no interest in waiting years to obtain the money that is, after all, rightfully his. But just because money rightfully belongs to someone else does not mean that you should not take it. If money is left on the table, it is fair game. If the creditor fails to take those legal steps necessary to protect his position, leave his money in your pocket. It may get to stay there.

17

Time

TIME IS MONEY, BUT MONEY IS NOT TIME. • NATURE DECAYS, BUT GOLD LASTS FOREVER. • TIME ERASES ALL DEBTS, SAVE THOSE OWED TO YOU. • TIME, LIKE GOLD, IS A HIGHLY LIMITED COMMODITY. • YOU CAN'T BUY FATE.

WHEN SO MUCH OF the service economy bills by the hour the truth of the saying "time is money" is easily seen. However, it is not a true equivalence. Money can help make time available: paying someone to cook your food, wash your clothes and clean your house frees up time that otherwise might be spent doing these things. Without money, time is always short.

While you cannot buy fate, you can diminish its effects with money. An ill person with money is able to purchase expensive treatments which might prolong life. You cannot prevent a disease from striking, but you can pay doctors for treatment.

Not enough people use the magic word, "no." It is the only word that can create time.

You may not be able to avoid a criminal conviction for your bad behavior, but you can afford expensive lawyers, lobbyists and publicists in an effort to get you off the hook. If you end up with a conviction, your money will make whatever consequence you face all that much easier to take. And while money may not directly buy luck, money can help put you in a situation where you are better situated to take advantage if luck indeed comes your way.

After ninety days, accountants tell business to mark down or even write off debt. A debt that has not been paid within a 90-day period, statistically speaking, will never be paid. Identify the debtor and move on. But if someone owes you money, never forget it. Don't write off personal debts owed to you. Sell them instead. And if the person who owes you money comes into good fortune, insist upon the repayment of the debt.

Statutes of limitations, as far as you are concerned, only work one way. Offer a discount if that will put funds from an otherwise unrecoverable debt into your pocket. In many jurisdictions, even a token payment on a debt will revive the statute of limitations, making formal collection procedures possible. The threat of such procedures is often more effective than their actual use.

Insist upon the "moral obligation" to repay the debt, even though you would not pay yourself in such circumstances. That others recognize this obligation is their problem, if they think they will get right with Jesus by paying you, don't get in their way by telling them it is no longer necessary. Put their money in your pocket.

18

Transactions

Never give money back. • The best deal is the one that earns the most money. • Opportunity costs are real. • Always exaggerate your estimates. • Never spend more than you have to. • There is no profit without secrecy. • You are not responsible for the stupidity of others. • The flimsier the product, the higher the price. • If you break it you've bought it. • Satisfaction is not guaranteed. • Never sell for less than you paid. • Never let the competition know what you're thinking. • Always know what you're buying. • Always inspect the merchandise before making a deal. • The more time they take deciding, the more money they will spend. • A bargain usually isn't. • Grant discounts sparingly. • Only a fool passes up a business opportunity.

. . .

The Grammar of Money

WARREN BUFFET'S "RULE NO. 1" is: Never lose money. His second rule is, "Never forget Rule No.1." All transactions must begin and end with these two rules in mind.

Negotiation is an art. You only think you know how to negotiate. Compared to the greats, even the experienced negotiator is just a beginner. A successful negotiation can be appreciated as any other sublime work of art or song.

Negotiating conduct varies from culture to culture. What is accepted in one culture is not necessarily accepted in another. I once told an Egyptian colleague that I needed to purchase a refrigerator. "Take me with you," he said, "I'll get you a better price." We walked into a shop and made our presence known. After a few pleasantries, the salesman happily quoted a price. "Can you tell me where you live?" the Egyptian asked him. "Why do you want to know?" answered the salesman. "Because tonight I will come to your house and kill you and your family for insulting me by quoting such a high, insulting price."

I was appalled but the salesman just laughed. In another country, the police might have been called. I watched the two professional negotiators laugh, threaten, cajole, weep and act out their parts. Eventually the desired discount came, but perhaps at a cost that few are really willing to pay. You do not have to threaten murder to get a discount, but everything is negotiable.

The children of immigrants to the United States are embarrassed when their parents ask for a discount in a fixed-price establishment. But here the parents know something the children do not: everything is negotiable. True, the salesman standing in front of you may not be able to secure the discount you desire, but there is always someone who can. If you can reach that person, you can negotiate.

The basic rule is that responsibility for the transaction falls on the buyer save for cases of outright fraud. If you buy a first edition of a rare book and fail to open its sealed packaging, you will have recourse if the box contains only a rock. But if you are offered only a rare book and assume that seller is selling the first edition and you find the much less-valuable second edition, you have no recourse. If the seller told you it was the first edition, yes, but if the seller only said that the book was valuable, you are out of luck. Thus the rule: always know what you are buying. Otherwise, you are throwing money away. A bargain is rarely what it seems.

19

Truth

THE BIGGER THE SMILE, THE SHARPER THE KNIFE. • KEEP YOUR LIES CONSISTENT. • THE BEST LIES ARE SEEDED WITH THE TRUTH. • WHEN IT'S GOOD FOR BUSINESS, TELL THE TRUTH. • NOT EVEN DISHONESTY CAN DIM THE SHINE OF PROFIT. • WHEN IN DOUBT, LIE. • IF YOU BELIEVE IT, THEY BELIEVE IT. • TRUTH AND BUSINESS ARE INCOMPATIBLE. • THE ONLY THING MORE DANGEROUS THAN A QUESTION IS AN ANSWER. • A GOOD LIE IS EASIER TO BELIEVE THAN THE TRUTH. • A GOOD LIE IS BETTER THAN THE TRUTH. • THERE'S NOTHING MORE DANGEROUS THAN AN HONEST BUSINESSMAN. • LYING IS JUST ANOTHER FORM OF COMMUNICATION.•

CHILDREN DO NOT HAVE to be taught how to lie, they know innately that a lie can provides protection from punishment. Instead, children are taught how to tell the truth and not to lie. One might well suppose that the innate human condition contains a natural predisposition to lies over truth. Otherwise, children would not need this instruction.

If lying is normative human behavior and telling the truth an aberration, lying should thus be the natural preferred course and the truth approached with caution as an unnatural, perverse practice.

Let's get one thing out of the way: there is no such thing as absolute truth. There is only your own truth, and this truth can change depending on the circumstances. If you believe your own truth to be other than what others believe, that is, the so-called "actual truth" you can still work on changing the mind of others to your side or simply ignore those inconvenient facts that highlight your own inconsistencies.

So much of life is deception. Business is deception, as the command *caveat emptor* shows. Benjamin Franklin believed that debt was worth than lies: "the second vice is lying, the first is running in debt." The Rule of Law should be renamed, the "Rule of Deception," as lawyers do little but create organized networks of lies.

What is an honest person? An honest person is merely someone whose truth is similar to your truth. That is all.

Liars tell you what they think you want to believe. Honest people tell you what they believe, even if what they believe has nothing to do with objective fact. The facts are always malleable; the reason why "fake news" is such an issue is because the means of distribution have been democratized so that accepted facts may now be more easily questioned. Talking back to the TV twenty years ago was a sign of dementia; now someone who posts his responses on social media may be followed by thousands.

Saddam Hussein's possession of weapons of mass destruction (itself a euphemism) was an instance of fake news sincerely believed by the chattering classes, by the mainstream media, but false, fake news nonetheless. Once credibility is lost, it is impossible to regain. In the wilderness of lies and false beliefs anyone's beliefs could be true, anyone's argument just as good as anyone else's. Once the truth is shown to be lies, your own truth, no matter how preposterous, becomes reasonable.

Courtrooms claim to be cathedrals of truth but in reality they are anything but. Evidence is suppressed, confessions are forced, documents redacted. Disclosure of information is restricted and perjury committed. Testimony is taken outside the presence of the jury to fit the prosecutor's preconceived narrative.

In these cathedrals, what is truth and what is a lie depend only on the caprice of twelve people pulled in off the street who don't want to be there. It is hardly a scientific method. Rather, it is instead a medieval torture chamber, ancient but no more accurate than any other process that dates from the 11th century. You would not trust 11th century science; you would certainly not trust 11th century medicine: so why would you trust the jury system?

"Because it is the best system we have," they say, while not explaining that no others, at least in the Anglo-American world of formal, commercial, rule of law justice, have ever been tried.

20

Wealth

SOMEONE ALWAYS HAS MORE MONEY. • ENOUGH IS NEVER ENOUGH. • REAL MONEY IS DISCREET. • MORE IS GOOD, EVEN MORE IS BETTER. • NEVER FLAUNT YOUR WEALTH. • SUDDEN WEALTH ALWAYS BRINGS UNEXPECTED CONSEQUENCES. • YOU MUST TRAIN FOR THE NEXT LEVEL. • WEALTH IS ITS OWN REWARD. • ONLY THOSE WITHOUT MONEY SAY THAT MONEY IS UNIMPORTANT. • BETTER TO CRY IN A BMW THAN LAUGH ON A BICYCLE. • MONEY ATTRACTS MONEY. • A WEALTHY MAN CAN AFFORD ANYTHING, EVEN A CONSCIENCE.

When Nathan Myerhold's Microsoft stock options suddenly became worth millions of dollars, he was awed by his new-found wealth. What to do with all of the money? One who had long flown in the upper-stratosphere of wealth told him, "what separates the truly wealthy from everyone else is an airplane. Buy yourself a jet."

In the film *Contact* the eccentric billionaire who funded the manufacture of the colossal dimensional spaceship used to travel through space-time to meet aliens lived permanently aboard a bespoke 727.

Owning an airplane is life-changing. The Internet meant the death of distance in the digital world, but having an airplane means that distance in real life world doesn't matter either.

If you hear about a hot new restaurant in a small town in Arkansas, you can call the jet and arrive in time for dinner. Airplanes are extraordinarily expensive and only the uber-wealthy can afford them. There are expenses upon expenses: FBO fees, landing fees, customs fees; not to mention the salaries of pilots (you will need at least three) and flight attendants. High net worth individuals do not plaster their names on the side of their aircraft, though they may dress the plane in corporate livery. True wealth is always discreet, never showy. Ultra high net worth individuals do not flex.

WITHOUT PROPER PREPARATION, sudden wealth can be a curse. Notorious B.I.G. pointed out, "the more money you make the more problems you get." He was not wrong. A study of lottery winners has shown that after only one year, most of them are broke. What happened? Those who do not understand the grammar of money are simply not ready for sudden wealth.

You can always move up one zero without too much difficulty but moving up two zero's is another matter. Moving up three or more is disconcerting.

Sudden wealth brings with it many unexpected consequences. First, of course, are all the freeloaders, charities and hard-luck story peddlers who are happy to divest you of some of your new-found wealth. These come in many guises and not all wear impoverished clothing. The most dangerous are those with well-tailored suits and ties. These wizards can transform safe investments into unprotected speculative, high risk and ultimately worthless holdings.

A person may know how to manage a household budget, balance a checkbook, make provisions for groceries and know which bills must be paid immediately and which ones can safely be put off. These skills are inadequate when great wealth is suddenly acquired. A foolish person who becomes wealthy is still a foolish person. The presence of money and its sycophants delude the fool into believing that all of a sudden he is wise. A windfall does not wisdom bring.

Galbraith pointed out that it is an error to mistake wealth for wisdom. The mistake is a natural one, since people want to enjoy the benefits of being wealthy. A wealthy person must have the secret sauce, must know the hidden path to wealth. A foolish person who becomes wealthy is still a foolish person.

If you are able to hold your wealth past the

first eighteen months you will then, and only then, start to reap the benefits of your new-found wealth. Beware of increasing your spending too fast: your nest egg will quickly diminish if you rely only on interest for replenishment. Savings accounts in Switzerland carry negative interest: don't even think of parking your money there.

One of the problems with a successful deal, or even a criminal score, is that by its nature it does not repeat. You have to understand this. With ten million dollars you can easily buy a two or three million dollar house, but unless your income continues at that ten million dollar level, in a few years that two or three million dollar house will eat up the rest of your holdings. There is a long line of former millionaires.

Money attracts money. When Bill Gates became a billionaire, he soon found that he was most comfortable in the company of other billionaires—not necessarily because of their wisdom, but simply because they did not ask anything of him. A common characteristic of the wealthy is loneliness. They are constantly on their guard. This leads to a withdrawal from society, from those with their hands out, from those with an agenda.

When a billionaire decides to "do good" for selfish reasons (since humanitarians rarely become billionaires), to expiate a perceived sin, or simply in order to have some human contact, to feel better about themselves, they quickly find that doing good only unleashes a horde seeking a handout. The needy network with each other. A donation to a charity triggers your placement on a donor list and more requests from similar charities. Donate to one politician and all his friends, colleagues and partisans will show no shame in asking you for cash too.

The wealthy are usually most happy when anonymous, in the company of those who have no idea of their wealth. This is not always easy to accomplish: it isn't easy hiding a Maybach in a parking lot full of Ford Escapes.

Those who have money know how important money is. It gives free reign to desire. No, money is desire itself.

But money is capricious, and earning it is a life-long endeavor informed by luck. It is impossible to be consistently lucky. Wealth takes many forms: people can inherit wealth, they can get lucky, a company can merge with another dragging along a lucky few to a higher level.

There is nothing wrong with trying to imitate the wealthy, but in doing so you will quickly find that you are living beyond your means. Living beyond your means takes a good deal of imagination, as Oscar Wilde pointed out. To be a successful in this regard you have to learn how to be a sponger without being a grifter. The minute you are seen as a grifter you will be shunned by the wealthy and excluded from their circles. They will inform each other to stay away, to keep you away. It is soul-crushing to find out that you have been excluded from the party, that your name is not on the private jet's manifest and that your seat has been taken by someone else.

A sponger, on the other hand, takes only when something is offered to him. He inserts himself into a position where he can accept if and only if something is offered. The truly wealthy will offer jobs. Someone who is performing a job can hardly be called a grifter, even if the result in the pocket is the same. There can be a fine line, though. Never step over it. When given the opportunity to fly high, remember your place. Perhaps you were elevated due to a whim, but you retain your position because of your talent. Remember that a whim can take you down just as fast and nothing would make your enemies happier than seeing you fall.

ABOVE ALL OTHER VIRTUES, the wealthy and powerful value loyalty in their subordinates. If you ever become wealthy, you will realize the value proposition that true loyalty brings. It is priceless.

And like anything else, loyalty can be bought.

Flatter the wealthy and the powerful. The wealthy and the powerful will remember your comments because they believe them. Many will say you can overdo flattery but this really isn't true. The wealthy and powerful believe the most extravagant flattery about themselves; they simply have found it impolite, in their rise to the top, to speak out loud what they believe to be true. You act as a proxy for their inner thoughts and they will not forget it. Others may hear these comments, moan and make a face, but if you look carefully at the target of your praise their features will not show rejection or disgust. Instead you will see only approval.

It is never a bad idea to have the wealthy and powerful on your side. You are the one who made the—in their mind at least—kind comments, while others said nothing. All things being equal, who is in the better position to benefit?

21

The Rules

General

- Money is everything.
- Nothing is more important than money.
- Money has no morality.
- Money is power.
- Money is frozen desire.
- Money is faith.
- Greed is an illusion.
- Greed is eternal.
- The lines separating vision, bullshit and fraud are narrow.
- Profit is its own reward.
- Anything worth doing is worth doing for money.
- It's always about the money.

Customers

- Don't tell customers more than they need to know.
- Learn the customer's weaknesses, so that you can better take advantage.
- Beware the customer's thirst for knowledge.
- All sellers are motivated.
- Cherish good customers.
- An angry customer is an enemy, and a satisfied customer is an ally.
- It's always good business to know about new customers before they walk in your door.
- Never cheat a customer unless you can get away with it.
- A paying enemy is a customer.
- Always help fools part with their money.
- Only fools pay retail.
- If you can't recognize the sucker at the table, you are the sucker.

Family and Friends

- Profit before family.
- Exploitation begins at home.
- Never place friendship above profit.

- Treat people in your debt like family…exploit them.
- Everything is for sale, even friendship.
- Beware of false partners.
- Every man has his price.
- Know your enemies and do business with them.
- Trust no one.
- Always put money over friendship; friendship rarely brings money.
- Business is business. If you want a friend, get a dog.

Honor

- A man with no money is no man at all.
- There is no honor in poverty.
- Hope doesn't keep the lights on.
- A man with an empty pocket and his dignity has an empty pocket.
- A poor man who still has his pride is a poor man.
- Let others keep their reputation. You keep their money.
- Morality is what is cost-effective.
- He who loses his money loses all.
- A man is only worth the sum of his possessions.

Law

- With money, laws can be changed.
- Justice delayed is justice achieved.
- Strive to be judgment proof.
- Possession is ownership.
- Pardons can be purchased.
- All sins are forgiven once you start making a lot of money.
- Money is always the reason for war.
- Vengeance is a luxury.

Love

- Love and finance don't mix.
- Trust is the biggest liability of all.
- A lover is a luxury, a smart accountant a necessity.
- Gold lasts longer than lust.

Management

- Employees are the rungs on the ladder of success. Don't hesitate to step on them.
- It's never too late to fire the staff.
- The less employees know about the cash flow, the less they can demand.

Misfortune

- Never confuse wealth with wisdom.
- When life hands you lemons, sell them.
- Theft is the penalty for failure to do due diligence.
- There is always someone happy to take your money.
- Trouble comes in threes.

Obligations

- A deal is a deal until a better one comes along.
- A contract is not always a contract.
- Contracts are written on sand.
- No agreement is binding.
- Betray to get a better deal.

Profit

- There are many paths to money.
- Sometimes the quickest way to find profits is to let them find you.
- Take joy from profit.
- Even in the worst of times someone turns a profit.
- Profit is its own justification.

- Never allow doubt to slow your pursuit of profit.
- Opportunity plus instinct equals profit.
- Flattery is necessary for success.
- War is good for business. Peace is good for business.
- The early investor reaps the most interest.
- Profit trumps emotion.
- Knowledge equals profit.

Real Property

- The American Dream has a useful life.
- Real estate is never more than an asset.
- The "For Sale" sign stays up after closing.
- Beware of those charging commissions.
- Appraisals are astrology.
- Staging is a skill for all interactions.
- Location, Location, Location.

Religion

- The God business is a business like any other.

- Some people doubt the existence of God, but no one doubts the existence of money.
- Only the rich can give to the poor.
- God cannot spend money.

Risk and Reward

- Risk doesn't always equal reward.
- Great risk may bring great profit.
- Small print leads to large risk.
- Danger awaits when things go well.

Self-Interest

- Always ask, "What's in it for me?"
- Always ask, "Am I going to get paid for this?"
- Good deeds are seldom profitable.
- There's nothing wrong with charity as long as it winds up in your pocket.
- There is no success without betrayal.
- Identify the enemy.

Strategy and Tactics

- Keep your eyes open.
- Hide your travels and your treasure.
- Choose no side but your own

- Never admit anything; always blame others.
- Expand or die.
- Better to ask for forgiveness than permission.
- Never ask when you can take.
- Always urge others to volunteer.
- Never get into anything that you can't get out of.
- Never rush to pay a debt.
- Listen to secrets, but never repeat them.
- Whisper your way to success.
- Always leave yourself an out.
- Buy when everyone else is selling and hold until everyone else is buying.
- Wait to bid until your opponents have exhausted themselves.
- Promise everything, deliver nothing.

Time

- Time is money, but money is not time.
- Nature decays, but gold lasts forever.
- Time erases all debts, save those owed to you.
- Time, like gold, is a highly limited commodity.
- You can't buy fate.

Transactions

- Never give money back.
- The best deal is the one that earns the most money.
- Opportunity costs are real.
- Always exaggerate your estimates.
- Never spend more than you have to.
- There is no profit without secrecy.
- You are not responsible for the stupidity of others.
- The flimsier the product, the higher the price.
- If you break it you've bought it.
- Satisfaction is not guaranteed.
- Never sell for less than you paid.
- Never let the competition know what you're thinking.
- Always know what you're buying.
- Always inspect the merchandise before making a deal.
- The more time they take deciding, the more money they will spend.
- A bargain usually isn't.
- Grant discounts sparingly.
- Only a fool passes up a business opportunity.

Truth

- The bigger the smile, the sharper the knife.
- Keep your lies consistent.
- The best lies are seeded with the truth.
- When it's good for business, tell the truth.
- Not even dishonesty can dim the shine of profit.
- When in doubt, lie.
- If you believe it, they believe it.
- Truth and business are incompatible.
- The only thing more dangerous than a question is an answer.
- A good lie is easier to believe than the truth.
- A good lie is better than the truth.
- There's nothing more dangerous than an honest businessman.
- Lying is just another form of communication.

Wealth

- Someone always has more money.
- Enough is never enough.
- Real money is discreet.
- More is good, even more is better.

- Never flaunt your wealth.
- Sudden wealth always brings unexpected consequences.
- You must train for the next level.
- Wealth is its own reward.
- Only those without money say that money is unimportant.
- Better to cry in a BMW than laugh on a bicycle.
- Money attracts money.
- A wealthy man can afford anything, even a conscience.

About the Author

From a young age, Felouz was schooled in the customs of the Levant before graduating to greed and the relentless pursuit of personal wealth. He attended the London School of Economics and visited the University of Chicago's Booth School of Business.

www.ingramcontent.com/pod-product-compliance
Lightning Source LLC
Chambersburg PA
CBHW052100110526
44591CB00013B/2290